I Am Deaf

Heather Hammonds

Contents

I Am Deaf

Clap your hands.

Can you hear the sound?

Some boys and girls

cannot hear very well.

Some boys and girls

cannot hear at all.

I cannot hear.

I am deaf.

My mom is deaf, too.

Signs and Letters

I can make **signs**
with my hands.
The signs are for words
and letters.
This is the sign for "yes."

I can make letters
with my fingers, too.
Here are some letters.

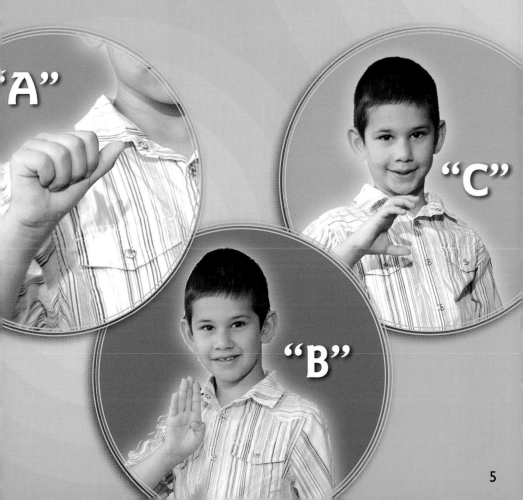

"A"

"C"

"B"

At School

Boys and girls
who cannot hear
go to my school.

We do lots of things
at my school.

Our teachers help us
to make things.
They help us
to read and write, too.

We make signs
with our teachers.

My Friend

My friend cannot hear very well.

He has **hearing aids**.

The hearing aids help him
to hear some sounds.

At Home

We have a light
on our doorbell,
at home.
Mom and I
cannot hear
the doorbell,
but we can see
the light on it.

Look at our telephone.

It is a little bit

like a computer.

My Friends

I like to look at the television.

I look at the pictures
and I read the words.

>> Come for a run, Scruffy. <<

Hello John,
How are you?

I can send an **e-mail**
to my friends.
Mom helps me
with some of the words.

Glossary

e-mail ——————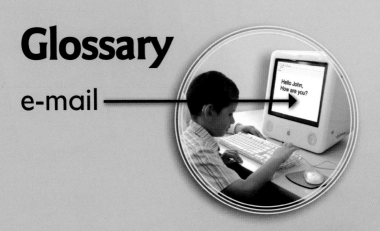

hearing aids ——————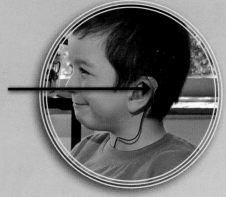

signs